Restless Humanity

by C. Truman Rogers

Editorial Offices: Glenview, Illinois • Parsippany, New Jersey • New York, New York
Sales Offices: Needham, Massachusetts • Duluth, Georgia • Glenview, Illinois
Coppell, Texas • Ontario, California • Mesa, Arizona

ISBN: 0-328-13600-X

3 4 5 6 7 8 9 10 V0G1 14 13 12 11 10 09 08 07 06

We often hear of someone who leaves his or her home country to come to the United States. We also hear about illegal immigrants—people who have left their countries to enter the United States without the government's permission. They are in danger of being sent back to their native countries because they have broken immigration laws.

Why do people persist in risking everything they have to come to an unfamiliar land? Why are they willing to travel, sometimes risking their lives, to go to an unknown destination? And how do immigrants adapt to their new lives, as they bring their skills and customs along with them? These are just some of the questions we'll explore as we learn about why and how people migrate.

A newly arrived immigrant family at Ellis Island in the early twentieth century

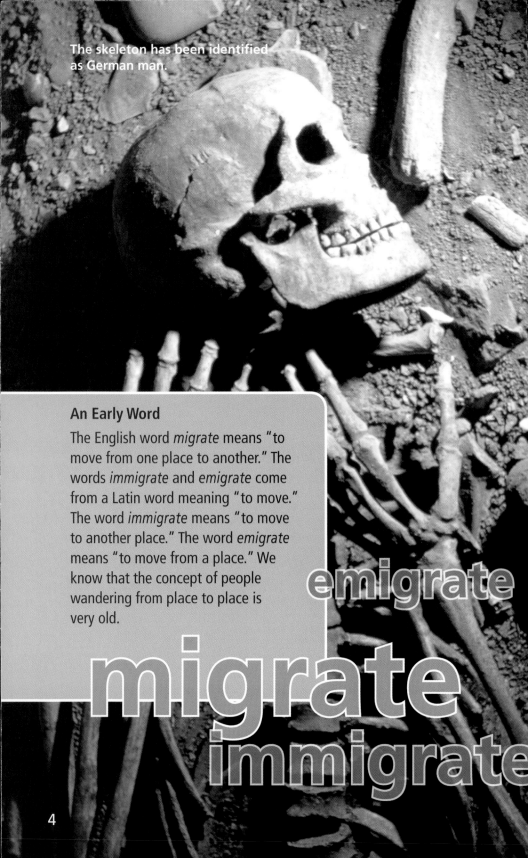

The skeleton has been identified as German man.

An Early Word

The English word *migrate* means "to move from one place to another." The words *immigrate* and *emigrate* come from a Latin word meaning "to move." The word *immigrate* means "to move to another place." The word *emigrate* means "to move from a place." We know that the concept of people wandering from place to place is very old.

emigrate

migrate

immigrate

Early Migration

Migration accounts for the spread of the human species over Earth for hundreds of thousands of years. The first migrants may have traveled northward from Africa into Asia and gradually made their way into central Europe. The oldest human fossil in Europe was found in Germany.

Early people hunted animals for meat, hides, and bones. They gathered plants, grains, and berries. When their food supplies became scarce, they moved in order to find other sources of food.

Early humans did not live in settled communities. More than likely, they lived in groups, perhaps sheltering in caves. They were not able to provide enough heat in times of extremely cold weather, so they would have had to move to places where the weather was warmer. Scientists now think that over the hundreds of thousands of years that human beings were establishing themselves in Europe, they moved southward when the weather became too cold and northward when the weather was warmer. They were not able to stay in any one area for long because of the great changes in temperature.

Early humans prepare food after a successful hunt.

In addition to the need to find food sources and a comfortable climate, competition became another strong factor influencing migration among groups of early people. As more humans occupied an area, competition for food became more intense. Stronger groups drove the weaker ones away, causing them to migrate elsewhere. In many ways, competition remained a reason for migration in the great modern movements of people.

The most basic reasons for migration have not changed over thousands of years. Even though the social organization of humans has become more and more complex, people today still migrate to find better places for themselves in other locations.

Anthropologists believe that early humans migrated into areas of Europe that are now part of France, Italy, and Austria and over a land bridge from Asia to North America.

This cave painting shows a hunting party.

Economy and Migration

For early humans, migration was a part of life—a group or family always knew they might have to move to find better fishing, larger herds of animals to hunt, or a milder climate.

By about 8,000 B.C., however, people had begun to farm. They did not have to move to find food; rather they had to stay in one place to take care of their farms. This great agricultural revolution brought huge changes to human social organization as people began to organize themselves into communities.

People who migrated did so because the land was no longer fertile or there was not enough rainfall. Taking their knowledge of agriculture with them, they became migrants with valuable skills that they could use elsewhere. They were migrants who elected to migrate based on economic opportunity.

Finding and harvesting food was always a valued skill.

The "Amesbury Archer" was found buried along with flint arrowheads in Amesbury, near Stonehenge, in Southwest England. Archaeologists believe the body came from what is now Switzerland. In the grave, archaeologists recently found another grave from the same period that contained people from Wales, which was also where the monument stones came from. It seems likely that workmen migrated from Wales to England to help build Stonehenge.

Archaeologists who have found gravesites near Stonehenge, England, guess that people from several different places may have been responsible for its construction.

Other Reasons for Migration

As the human population grew, people formed communities, and the social organization became much more complicated, leading to the development of local governments. Such organization was needed to prevent violent competition for the necessities of life that could bring danger or outright warfare.

Of course, there were people who could not or would not live in the manner that the rest of their tribe or

Soon after Columbus sailed to the New World, there were several great religious migrations in Europe.

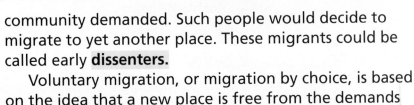

community demanded. Such people would decide to migrate to yet another place. These migrants could be called early **dissenters.**

Voluntary migration, or migration by choice, is based on the idea that a new place is free from the demands of the old place. Also, people move to another place as a **refuge** from a society that cannot accept differences. This reason for migration is extremely old and remains a major reason for migration today.

For many years, the Moors controlled most of the territory that is now Spain. The Spanish began to take back their country little by little and finally, in 1492, achieved complete control. The new rulers were not **tolerant** of different religions, however, and they gave the Moors and the resident Jews a choice: convert to Christianity or get out. Finally, about 300,000 Moors and 150,000 Jews were expelled from Spain.

This is the Alhambra, the beautiful and famous palace of the Spanish Moors.

Where did the Moors and Jews go when they left Spain? The Jewish people migrated largely to England, France, and to the Ottoman Empire (now Turkey). The Moors went to North Africa.

Religious migration did not take place only in Spain during the 1500s to the mid-1700s. In France and the Netherlands at this time, people were migrating for religious reasons. They migrated mainly within Europe. If they went where they could practice their religion without **harassment,** they tended to stay.

The freedom to practice one's religion also caused a wave of migration to North America. By the time Europeans were beginning to move to the Americas in large numbers, however, they had other reasons to leave. Europe was crowded, and space was limited, as were resources. Competition for employment increased. So another wave of migration occurred—this time more for economic reasons than for religious reasons. Sometimes the governments of the European countries encouraged people to leave for the Americas. England, France, Holland, and Spain were all eager to establish colonies in North and South America so that they could have access to the natural riches of those continents. By 1776, when the United States declared its independence from Britain, the population of the country was made up of millions of people— every one of them an immigrant or a descendant of immigrants.

Notable Migrations

1492: Nearly 500,000 religious refugees left the Iberian Peninsula

1570: Catholics and some Protestants left England

1578: Protestants moved from Southern Netherlands into Belgium and Nordic countries

Early 1600s: 200,000 French Huguenots left France

1626: Thousands of Scandinavians began migrating to other European countries

1650–1750: Jews migrated to England

1685: 200,000 French fled to England, Switzerland, the Rhineland, and the Dutch Republic

1691: Irish migrated to France

The First Americans

We know that Europeans were not the first people to migrate to North America. More than 10,000 years ago, people from Asia migrated to North America. Scientists believe that at that time, the North American continent was attached to Asia by a land bridge across the Bering Sea. This bridge was probably at the tip of what is now Alaska, and people may have followed animal herds to an area now called Beringia.

When the last Ice Age ended and the great glaciers melted, the land bridge became covered with water.

Ancient Native American migration spread in settlements throughout the Western Hemisphere. There Native Americans split into different groups and developed different customs and languages.

Some scholars believe, based on similarities in languages, that such a migration happened three separate times.

Early immigrants followed elk, moose, and horses over the land bridge to the grasslands of Beringia.

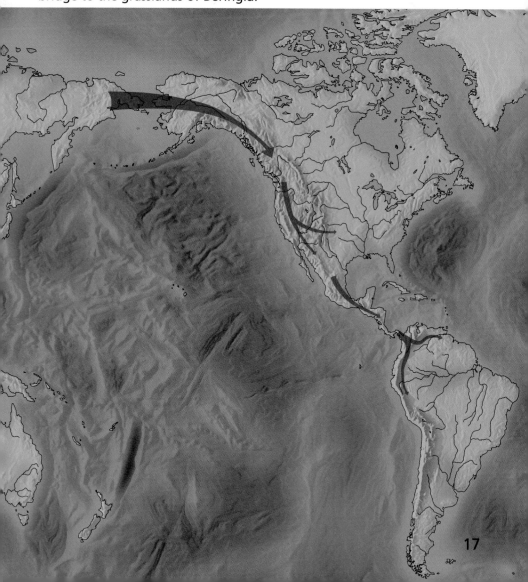

War and Migration

War is another cause of migration. In earlier times, the march of an army through an area caused great hardship for the inhabitants, as soldiers stole food, cattle, and valuable possessions from people as they passed through their land. Modern warfare is also a cause for people to flee.

During World War II, bombings made some cities unlivable, causing a wave of migration after the war.

One of the greatest migrations took place during World War II (1938–1945), which pitted the Axis (Germany, Italy, and Japan) against the Allies (the United States, England, Canada, Australia, Russia, and others). While the fighting was going on, civilians tried to flee to safety. Once the war was over, huge numbers of people migrated back to their homelands. Others elected to migrate to other countries. Still others were forced to move when borders were redrawn and people were expelled from what had been "their" lands. Some enthusiastically migrated to establish the new country of Israel as a homeland for the Jewish people.

Many boats brought immigrants to Israel after the devastation of Europe in World War II.

People continue to migrate because of conflict and governmental change in their countries. They also migrate because of poverty and lack of economic opportunity in their homelands. They leave homelands with their hearts filled with hopes for a better, safer life. The need for people to have enough food, security, and a job is so great that they decide to undertake the extremely challenging task of migrating to an unknown place.

Groups of people from Cuba and other countries have come to the United States in small boats, risking their lives to escape conflict at home.

New arrivals in the United States often work during the day and take English classes at night.

Settling

Settling in a new nation involves many adjustments, for everything is different—the culture, the laws, the educational system, and the language. Many immigrants, hoping for social **stability,** move to areas where people from their homelands have already settled. Groups of earlier immigrants and community organizations help the new arrivals.

Regardless of the difficulties of migration, people continue to do it. As we have seen, even with the passage of time, the reasons for migration are remarkably similar. Like our prehistoric ancestors, today's immigrants make adjustments and face a restless search for a better place to live.

Now Try This

The story of human migration is a story of great courage and determination. All migration requires a person to give up what is familiar to live where everything is unfamiliar. Here are some ideas of things to do that might make the act of migration more real to you.

Choose one of the following scenarios. You will need to do some research to finish your project, but choosing where and how to do your research might prove a challenge. You can ask your teacher or librarian for help in getting started.

F.E.D.E

דבהות

Here's How to Do It!

1. You are living in Spain in the 1500s. You are a metalworker who fashions beautiful metal objects. You had a good business, but now you are poor. You decide to migrate. Where would you go? How would you get there? What would you take with you? Try to plan your migration.

2. You are a local community leader. You know that many immigrants have settled in your town. You also know that they could use help in settling into their new communities. How would you get your friends and other members of the community to help? What kinds of help would you try to provide? Where would you look to find information on your topic?

3. In your community, there are probably people who have come from other countries. Ask to interview some of them. Ask questions about why they came and how long it took for them to begin to feel comfortable. Find out if they had any help either coming to this country or settling into a community.

4. Make a time line that shows the migration paths of two or three different groups during a specific time period. Use this book to help you, or use your school's library resources.

Glossary

dissenters *n.* persons who refuse to agree with an established religion, culture, or community

harassment *n.* conduct that tends to annoy, alarm, or abuse another person

refuge *n.* a place that gives safety or security

stability *n.* permanence, firmness

tolerant *adj.* willingness to recognize and respect the beliefs of others